Carine
Gilson

Garden of Lace

LANNOO

Cover pictures
Calla Lily, 1995-2001, © Tom Baril
Tamara, Fall-Winter 2012, © Xavier Harcq

Endpapers
Drawing *Garden of Lace*, Spring Summer 2020,
© Maison Carine Gilson

TABLE OF CONTENT

PREFACE

Karen Van Godtsenhoven
HH Al Reem Al Tenaiji

6

I
CURIOUSER AND CURIOUSER

Karen Van Godtsenhoven

10

II
SILK AND LACE

Caroline Esgain & Catherine Gauthier

42

MON COEUR EST FAIT DE DENTELLE

Karen Van Godtsenhoven

86

III
ATELIER

104

LACE-INCRUSTED SILK IS MY HANDWRITING

Caroline Esgain

121

THE TROUSSEAU

Caroline Esgain & Catherine Gauthier

131

VI
A GARDEN OF HER OWN

Karen Van Godtsenhoven

144

'But I don't want to go among mad people,'
Alice remarked.
'Oh, you can't help that,' said the Cat:
'we're all mad here. I'm mad. You're mad.'
'How do you know I'm mad?' said Alice.
'You must be,' said the Cat,
'or you wouldn't have come here.'

Lewis Carroll,
Alice's Adventures in Wonderland, 1865

PREFACE

Karen Van Godtsenhoven

Kirsten Dunst gazes at us with an indomitable spirit of female sovereignty. She is dressed in an ensemble of silk and lace, signed Carine Gilson. Although she reclines, classically, like Manet's Olympia, her gaze is one of dominion, haloed by platinum curls à la Jean Harlow. She exists in her own world and languishes in her own reverie. Her bare, porcelain-hued skin, overlaid with the fabrics, touches itself. The rippled cream silk is edged with floral arabesques of black lace, demarcating the transition from the fabric to the human flesh. Lace is the muse which inspires the work of Gilson, who breathes a world of inspiration into her work and sustains her daily acts of creation. While her work invites us to dream, by evoking mysterious lands and ethereal skies, it is also a labour of patience and constancy, and forever beginning anew, like the long hours of Penelope who would weave by day and unravel the fabric by night. Like the wise Ariadne, making sure she always has enough thread to find her way back out of the maze, Gilson solves the puzzle with her imagination. It is in this long tradition of women working through fabric and thread, labouring daily with painstaking exactness, with an adventurous spirit and a touch of madness, that Gilson's work comes into being.

PREFACE

HH Al Reem Al Tenaiji

It is such an honour and a privilege to have been asked by Carine to write the foreword for this beautiful book.

I first became aware of Carine's designs in 2014. Her Pont Street shop in London's Knightsbridge district sits just a few paces from my hairdresser. One day I found myself pausing by a glorious window display of midnight-hued silks edged with the finest lace, drawn into a world of elegance and glamour. I remember trying on one of her pieces: a butterfly-sleeved Chantilly lace kimono in duck-egg blue. Handmade – like all of her designs – it floated effortlessly to the floor and conjured such a rich vision and feeling that I knew immediately I had found something special.

I was soon lucky enough to meet Carine – a graceful woman with amazing energy and an open heart – on a visit to the United Arab Emirates. We clicked instantly. After hearing about her history, her ideas and her inspiration, I felt certain that we should work on a project together; one to empower and enrich the lives of women all over the world. She was, and continues to be, a joy to work with.

Carine's aesthetic approach, based on her motto 'Everything is a paradox', perfectly encapsulates what it is to be a woman: strong yet feminine, beautiful, intuitive and at our most powerful moment when empowering others. Her pieces are not designed for the outside world, but for ourselves, our closest connections. It is self-care in its purest form.

Carine is a storyteller. Her signature lace pattern – the Garden of Eden – evokes an awareness of romance and abundance; an inner peace gifted from a higher place. It is a story I have followed in my own life and work.

This book is a tribute and testament to the art of working with lace, and the imagination and rare skills, passed down from generation to generation, needed to become a true master.

'The chief difficulty Alice found at first was in managing her flamingo', 1865, John Tenniel, first edition of *Alice's Adventures in Wonderland*

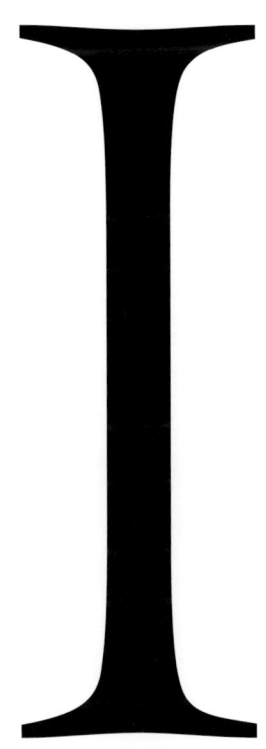

CURIOUSER AND
CURIOUSER

Photograph from the *Beauty and the Beast* collection, 1995,
© Stéphane Borremans, model Germaine

Alice laughed. 'There's no use trying,' she said. 'One can't believe impossible things.'

'I daresay you haven't had much practice,' said the Queen. 'When I was your age, I always did it for half-an-hour a day. Why, sometimes I've believed as many as six impossible things before breakfast.'

Lewis Carroll,
Alice's Adventures in Wonderland, 1865

CURIOUSER AND CURIOUSER

Karen Van Godtsenhoven

Growing up in Brussels in the 1970s, Carine Gilson, a high-spirited young girl, was surrounded by the beautiful fabrics her mother worked with in her tailoring atelier where she produced made-to-measure two-piece suits, dresses, blouses and coats for the ladies of the upper middle class. These clients would have their clothes custom-made so they would fit like a glove, both hugging and shaping the body. They were sophisticated and stern. Gilson's mother had a predilection for expensive fabrics, for the most resplendent materials ranging from supple jerseys to fragile lace. She and her daughter would shop for these fabrics together in large warehouses and take patterns from different magazines. Teaching Carine to distinguish between different qualities, she instilled in her an understanding of how to assess a fabric, how to make it move between her fingers, to feel its 'fall', its suppleness and weight, its tactile qualities which would, when the fabric became a garment, embrace the body – a sixth sense that unites the coordination of hand and eye with a sensuous imagination and capacity for wonder. She also instilled a sense of independence in her precocious daughter, of literally taking things into her own hands, giving the twelve-year-old Carine not just permission but the patterns, tools and materials with which to make her own clothes, hitherto made by her. Armed with an eagerness to learn and a can-do attitude, Gilson thenceforth proceeded to make and wear all her own clothes.

Although her mother's work was based on the cutting and sewing techniques that are the basis of tailoring (used for daywear), rather than what in couture terms is referred to *le flou* (draping and sewing around the body, mostly used for evening wear), it was the fluid, sensual silks and diaphanous laces typical of *flou* that beguiled Gilson. She was mesmerized by the intimate underdresses worn between the body and the outer dress, which spoke to her in a language of emotions and conveyed a sense of curiosity.

Beauty and the Beast, Spring-Summer 1995,
© Stéphane Borremans, model Germaine

Later she taught herself to work with silk in this way, by honouring the material and listening to it: 'It is the material which has taught me, I just had to learn what it had to say. By touching silk and being attentive to its character, the material teaches you how to work her. If you don't listen well she responds with a folded grimace.' That sense of dialogue and learning, of being tempted and taught by touch, remains with Gilson to this day.

Her early imagination was also fuelled by the glamorous sirens of the 1950s silver screen, who wore silk slips beneath conservative daywear: scenes of Hitchcock actresses removing a garment and revealing the slip underneath imprinted in Gilson the desire for working on garments which symbolized an exalted femininity, a femininity *par excellence*, as conveyed by the languorous Sophia Loren, the statuesque Grace Kelly and the mysterious and enchanting Marlene Dietrich. The 'slip dress' was the spark that fired Gilson's imagination, or, as she muses today, 'It was a superb slip dress that started it all.'

In the 1980s, the epitome of seductive, ladylike femininity was not synonymous with the epitome of fashion, with its mixture of broad-shouldered, corporate women, its casual sportswear and the advent of unisex, androgynous clothing by the conceptual designers from Japan and Belgium. During this time, Gilson spent three years studying Fashion Design at the Royal Academy of Fine Arts in Antwerp under teachers like Linda Loppa and Walter Van Beirendonck, who taught her how to create a collection with a strong concept and structured approach and to present it in a way that conveyed a coherent artistic DNA. Gilson was shaped by this approach and it is still with her today: 'In a way, the critical and regular jury moments at the Academy prepared me for the harsh rhythm of the fashion cycle: each collection today is like a jury moment, with the buyers and clients filling the role previously held by the teachers.' The Antwerp Academy fashion department is famed for its high standards and pursuit of excellence, for pushing its students to constantly re-evaluate themselves and, if need be, to start again from scratch. Even though Gilson's aesthetic was different at the time from the school's artistic direction, her years there created space for self-discovery and perseverance, leading to her credo that 'Nothing is impossible. Perseverance makes things possible.' Her self-affirming attitude is best expressed in her own mother tongue: 'Rien n'est impossible, il faut y croire.'

Orientalisme, Spring-Summer 1996,
© Stéphane Borremans, model Germaine

L'après-midi d'un faune, Fall-Winter 1997,
© Stéphane Borremans, model Milou

With the fashion design course completed, Gilson set forth on the path of self-determination. At the age of twenty-two (just ten years after starting to 'do things on her own') she persuaded the bank to grant her a loan that would enable her to take over a faltering lace incrustation atelier in Brussels with four employees. She had to work hard to gain the respect of the older employees, but she was young and fearless. And when they grasped her palpable vision of 'lingerie couture' and the creative possibilities it brought to their practice of lace incrustation – whereby the lace is set into the garment, covering a negative space, rather than being applied to the fabric – they went along on the novel adventure with their new *patronne*, Mademoiselle Carine.

Gilson learned the eight *métiers* or types of craftsmanship that comprise the techniques of haute couture by instinct and the pursuit of perfection. For even though she trained at the Academy she could also be called self-taught, having learned by 'looking and daring' to create the garments she dreamed of in a vision that was uniquely personal and unheard of. Painstakingly, she discovered how to incrust lace on patterns cut on the bias (diagonal to the weave of the fabric), sometimes having to start over again, losing valuable lace. 'One has to learn how to tame the lace and make it do what you want, and this takes up a lot of time,' Gilson smiles. 'Restarting and trying again is part of my process, I like to observe and to learn from my mistakes.' She does not start with cotton toiles but always works directly with the silks and laces, as cotton lacks the fluidity of silk and the lace needs to go directly onto the silk. This is both exhilarating and gratifying to Gilson, whose emotional sensibility makes her her own best judge in deciding whether a piece 'talks' or enters into a dialogue with the body: 'I have to understand the piece. When the piece does not talk, one has to be able to throw it out. Like that time everything had to go one week before the presentation of the collection.'

Patience and an unhurried approach seem to be the pre-eminent virtues for those working with lace, but this runs contrary to the machine-like rhythm of fashion, that Minotaur-like beast which demands a new collection every three months. It pushes Gilson towards new territories, which suits her can-do energy. When she was twenty-three, having been at the helm of her own company for only a short time, she approached the best fabric suppliers in Lyon (silk) and Chantilly (lace), asking whether she could buy their

Hand-painted silk slip dress, *Russian Ballets*, Spring-Summer 1997, © Stéphane Borremans, model Milou

prized goods. She was met with the same sort of questions as when she asked for a loan from the bank: What are you doing here? Who are you? How will you pay for these goods upon delivery? And, just as in the bank, she enthusiastically explained her vision of lingerie couture – and acquired a small piece of Chantilly lace.

As anyone in the fashion business will tell you, entering the different production areas as a small designer with small quantities and no credit history to speak of is no easy matter. So, for the first ten years Gilson focused on her product, on doing things that went against the grain of what was happening, doing them in a way that they were no longer being done, reviving what had been lost, refabricating what had been lying dormant because it was not profitable. She sees it as a sort of birthing process of a niche product which initially held no attractions for investors because it was not (directly) profitable. Ahead of the curve in terms of the appreciation of slow processes and high-quality niche products, Gilson saw the real value of luxury in the very fact that it was a niche product slowly made.

The creative appeal of Gilson's lingerie couture was picked up early on by the American high-end department store Barneys, her first client, who understood the market for this luxury product, a market that existed at first in the Middle East and the United States. They nurtured her talent and pushed her to go further, be bolder in her approach to creating a niche product, lingerie made and incrusted with lace by hand. A challenge, certainly, to create a product, whose timelessness is its strength and which alters with the seasons ever so slightly. Like minimal music, Gilson's work repeats patterns and themes, in an endless quest for perfection. Refining and reworking pieces from her own thirty-year archive she has therefore created a new line, *Les Intemporelles*, based on those iconic pieces whose relevance is timeless, pieces for which her clients return again and again, that make up the DNA of her universe. In the decade to come, Gilson wants to keep using those models and their patterns, as time has proven their significance.

Almost ironically, Gilson does not appear in the official haute couture Parisian calendar because of its stringent, location-based conditions, although she uses couture techniques in her Brussels atelier. Shying away from the fashion scene, she is one of the few people today working away in the mode of the couturiers of bygone

An Ethereal Temptation

p. 30-31 Contact sheet from the 25th anniversary, *Jardin de Paradis* collection, Fall-Winter 2015, © Stéphane Borremans, model Kim Peers

l'Envol, Fall-Winter 2019, © Stéphane Borremans, model Ana

times, in the silence of her atelier. Yet her contribution does not go unrecognized and her intrepid spirit has made her long-cherished girlhood dream come true: to develop her own signature lace in collaboration with the renowned French lace atelier Sophie Hallette, based in Caudry, France. With that house, founded in 1887 by Eugene Hallette, Gilson shares the *esprit du nord*, the will to venture ever further, industriousness, self-determination, groundedness. They also share a heart full of passion for lace, since people who work with lace might look at the world in a different way, a way that puts beauty, a slow approach and materials first.

For her signature lace pattern, Gilson has turned to her own inner 'Garden of Eden of lace' and created a floral motif which hovers on the brink between Art Nouveau and Art Deco, two styles which have put a strong mark on Belgian architecture and design and which have inspired her since her early days. Serpentine in her scrolls, rich in detail and difficult to create, the flower of the pattern is sublime and beautiful, an exquisite example of the Keatsian notion of beauty as 'a joy forever'. With her own lace pattern, Gilson creates an affirmative statement which at once propels her expertise and heritage into the future and protects her work from those who would copy it. It is her way of tending her own garden of lace and preserving it for the future.

Cérès, Pre-Fall-Winter 2016,
© Stéphane Borremans, model Joy

Hand-pleated lace dress, Éphémère, Fall-Winter 2019
Evening, © Stéphane Borremans, model Joy

p. 40-41 Contact sheet from the *L.A. Confidential* collection, Fall-Winter 1994, © Stéphane Borremans

Marlène Dietrich, Cecil Beaton,
© The Cecil Beaton Studio at Sotheby's

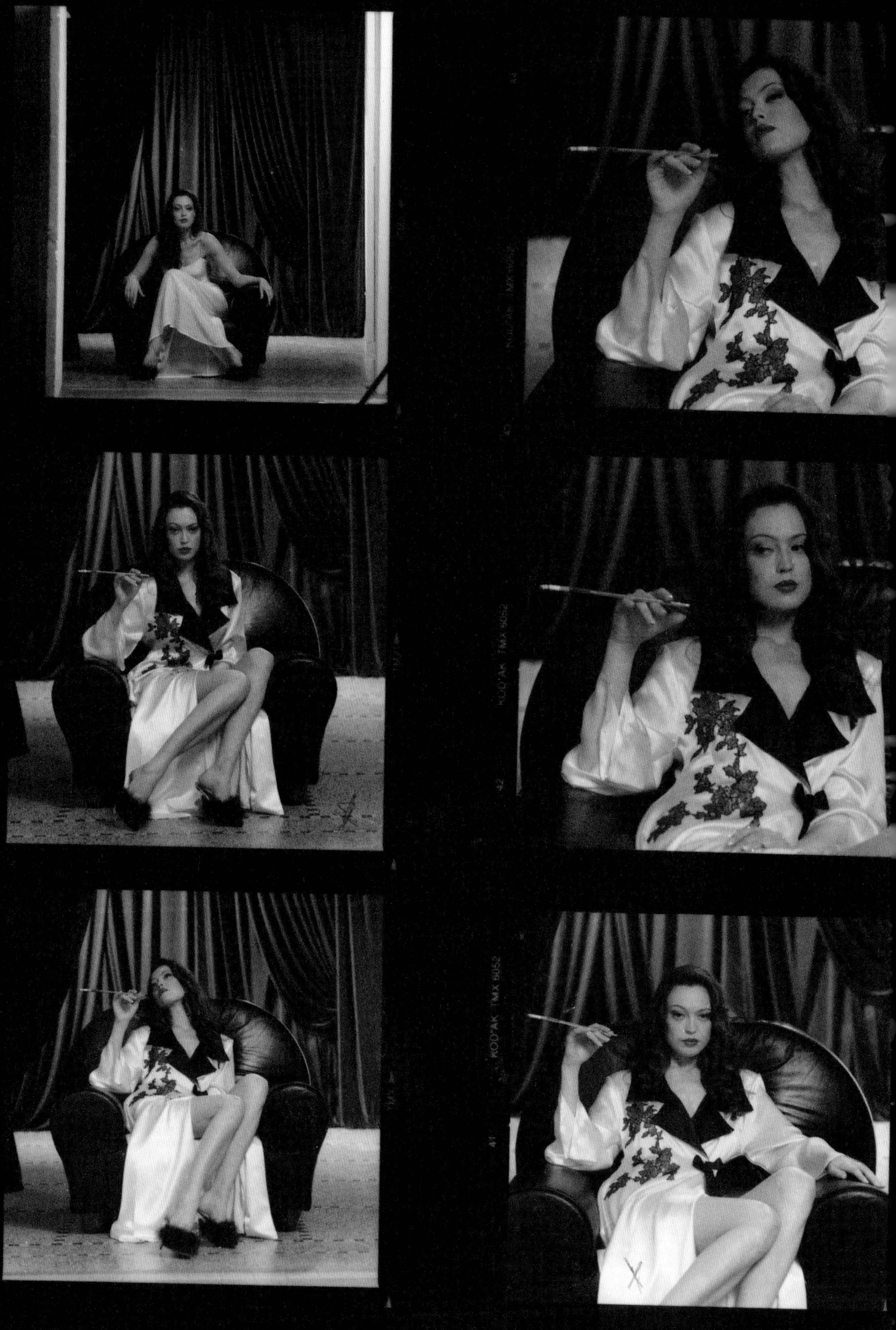
KODAK TMX 6052

II

SILK & LACE

l'Envol, Fall-Winter 2019,
© Stéphane Borremans, model Ana

SILK AND LACE

Caroline Esgain & Catherine Gauthier
Curators at the Fashion & Lace Museum in Brussels

Carine Gilson's creativity is expressed mainly through the mediums of silk and lace. These are the materials she cherishes and returns to time and again, understanding them thoroughly and masterly in their handling. Fashion designers and stylists rarely adhere so strictly to just one or two preferred materials. The diversity of textiles available is, after all, virtually unlimited – a lack of restriction that often leads them to employ a broad range allowing for infinite variation. Yet perhaps it is that very selectivity that has enabled Gilson to maintain her own brand in Brussels uninterruptedly for three decades – no mean feat in the world of contemporary fashion design. Which is why we propose to present the Belgian stylist's work by focusing on her chosen materials: silk and lace. We will see how lace and incrustation work have fascinated her ever since she rebooted the manufacture of slip dresses in 1989. How she elevated incrustation to the level of artistic craftsmanship, which has become her signature mark. How silk and lace are the vocabulary for her primary mode of expression, renewed with every new collection yet always ensuring that 'she'll find her own path through lace'. And last but not least, we will establish exactly where Carine Gilson fits in the history of Brussels lace, a luxury fabric *par excellence*, even though its swan song was already starting to be heard in the early twentieth century.

IN THE BEGINNING THERE WAS LACE

To fully grasp the intensity of her rapport with her working material, you should be fortunate enough to watch Carine Gilson looking at a piece of lace, eyes shining with admiration as she deftly examines the lacework, mesmerized by the delicate beauty of the patterns. She has a thorough understanding of lace patterns. Progressively, the motifs reveal to her the path she has to follow, consisting of

flowery meanders, branches, leaves, a fullness and an emptiness. You and I would not see it, but Gilson does. It will involve cut-outs, incrustations and openwork. Lace is and will forever be her muse.

Gilson sources her lace fabrics in the Hauts-de-France region, legendary nexus of machine lace, a lace-making method perfected there in the early nineteenth century. She sources the finest pieces of Chantilly lace, woven on Leavers looms by traditional Calais-Caudry®-labelled suppliers, which means she can choose from the thousands of types of lace that have been produced there during 200 years of manufacture. She will select one that inspires her and that fits with the theme of her upcoming collection. That theme and its associated mood board give each collection its specific identity and consist of a printed fabric, a range of colours and a lace pattern, all of which receive a unique name. These stages – choosing the print, choosing the lace pattern, choosing the colours – comprise the Gilson dialectics: everything is still there, but not necessarily in the same order.

FROM COMPOSITION TO INCRUSTATION

Next, Gilson embarks on the path she had perceived, intuited, mapped out. The twist she intends to give the material will take shape on the items of clothing themselves. The initial lace strip is cut, reviewed, restructured and reinvented to correspond with this novel twist. It is Gilson who decides where and how to attach the lace to the silk and what its incrustation should look like. This stage of the process is hers and hers alone to determine.

First, the paper reproduction is cut out and positioned on a dress form in order to create the desired pattern. Once the right motif has been established, the same process is repeated with real lace, arranged on a silk toile. A toile is a model for a finished garment. It allows the designer to judge its style and/or whether the desired effect can be achieved, before it is cut in the definitive fabric. Though a toile is generally made up in cotton, Gilson always uses silk, to anticipate as accurately as possible how the garment will ultimately drape.

Next, a second layer of lace is added, to allow for some playful incrustations and more subtle openwork. The superimposed layers

Detail from a negligee, *l'Envol*, Fall-Winter 2019, © Maison Carine Gilson

Detail from a long caftan, *l'Envol*, Fall-Winter 2019, © Maison Carine Gilson

of lace are almost imperceptible to the casual observer. Finally, the openwork is added: the silk fabric behind the lace is cut out. The result is always striking: it looks so simple and self-evident! And yet it takes two years to train an embroiderer to execute such delicate incrustation work.

The toile is now finished. Shortly we shall see how silk and lace harmonize in the newly composed patterns, how these two materials intertwine. At this point, the model is ready to go into production, manufactured by the expert workshop seamstresses. A maximum of around one hundred pieces per design will be produced here, entirely by hand.

Lacework is essential to Gilson's work. The openwork obtained by partially or completely excising the lace's silk backing is typical of incrustation. Moreover, the lacework often complements the print. Sometimes, the openwork forms a symmetrical transparent framework. The inverted pattern created by the interstices structures the final product, as can be seen in her exquisite incrusted kimonos, for instance.

For each collection Gilson uses a single lace pattern which she recomposes in every sense of the word. The pattern is cut out, embroidered, enlarged … Her instinct leads her to select the type of lace she prefers. Each one has a name and the colour of the silk associated with it is named after an object or concept related to the theme of the upcoming collection.

'SILK IS SOFT, SENSUAL, NOBLE.'
CARINE GILSON

Silk is not only the support for the lace, of course; it also determines the garment's feel.
From the very beginning, Gilson has been using the most beautiful silks. A privileged relationship has been established with Bucol, a producer of high-end fabrics from Lyon, internationally renowned among fashion houses. For each collection she consults Bucol's centuries-old archives to find the fabric that meets her requirements and ensures a perfect match with the lace she has selected. Sometimes new fabrics are created specially to order for her, as was the case for the remarkable collection *Les Tubéreuses* from the

Detail from a long kimono, *Cérès*, Pre-Fall-Winter 2017, © Maison Carine Gilson

Detail from a slip dress, *Lost in Wonderland*, Fall-Winter 2016, © Maison Carine Gilson

Detail from a long gown and a kimono, *Tubéreuse*, Fall-Winter 2018, © Maison Carine Gilson

2018-2019 autumn-winter collection, for which the pattern of a jacquard weave from the archives of Maison Bucol was revised and printed on the silk in three different versions.

Vibrant and alive, these silks 'work', and when a different material – in this case lace – is imposed on them and inserted into the weave, it's essential to be aware of how they will react. They will ripple, stretch or shrink according to changes in temperature and humidity and depending on how they have been cut. So they must rest before the lace incrustation is applied. It takes time to subdue the materials. The satins, *charmeuses* (a lighter type of satin), crepes and muslins are cut on the bias, which is technically more complex but gives the garment a much lighter hang when worn.

The prints are named according to the collection's theme: Jardin d'Eden (*Garden of Eden*), Jardin du Paradis (*Paradise Garden*), Sketch of Paradise, Garden of Lace, Lost in Wonderland, Tubéreuse bleue (*Blue Tuberose*), Blue, Tubéreuse rouge (*Red Tuberose*). The names of the plain fabrics also evoke the colours of nature: Acacia, Mist, Bruyère (*Heather*), Orpiment, Magnolia, Bleu Vénitien (*Venetian Blue*), Écume (*Foam*).
The lace fabrics are labelled Égérie (*Muse*), Venise (*Venice*), Cérès (*Ceres*), Florence, Julia, Florilège (*Florilegium*), Antoinette, Rosa, Alba, Anna, Éphémère (*Ephemeral*), Tamara.

CARINE GILSON'S PLACE IN THE HISTORY OF LACE

In 2017, the Fashion & Lace Museum asked Carine Gilson to act as godmother to its new permanent exhibition space, dedicated to the history of Brussels lace. From the mid-seventeenth to the early twentieth century, Brussels was a centre of lacemaking, producing a type of lace that was valued for its sophistication by all the royal courts in Europe. In this context, Carine Gilson is continuing a tradition of luxurious lace in the European capital, as all her designs are manufactured exclusively in her Brussels ateliers. She was certainly the right person to mentor the museum's Lace Room.

In 2019, the *Beautiful Lace & Carine Gilson* exhibition at the Fashion & Lace Museum celebrated thirty years of design and development of her couture lingerie – the first retrospective of her

oeuvre ever held. It not only gave Gilson the perfect opportunity to explore the museum's exceptional lace collection but also for her designs to dialogue with the pieces the museum holds. She also began to examine the various uses of lace. Who wore it? How was it worn? Did it embellish underwear right from the start? Was it more often worn on top of the clothes or underneath? Where was it made?

ON TOP AND UNDERNEATH, A LITTLE HISTORY OF (WEARING) LACE.

Lace was invented more or less simultaneously in Flanders and Venice in the mid-sixteenth century. It decorated the dress of both men and women and adorned the costumes of the elite. Individual items of lace, such as collars, cuffs, cravats, flounces and headwear, were ostentatiously added to the outer garments. Unlike a fabric woven on a loom, with warp and weft threads, lace was originally made with bobbins or needles – generally speaking the former in Flanders, the latter in Venice. Though the distinction may sometimes be blurred, this still gives us a suitable starting point from which to approach this complex field. Linen was the preferred material, since flax was cultivated and available in both regions.

In the second half of the seventeenth century, lace became increasingly typical of the place where it was made. Lace-producing centres like Brussels, Mechelen and Valenciennes, for instance, evolved recognizably specific characteristics, to the point where the lace and the place were synonymous. The fame of Brussels lace was built on luxury bobbin lace made by the part-lace process (the work was split between several individual lace-makers and the pieces they produced were then joined together). This had the advantage of speed, being faster than the bobbin technique with its continuous threads, and of facilitating the production of large pieces.

The eighteenth century was the golden age of handmade lace in the Low Countries. It was worn by both men and women and its quality was an indicator of their social status. But the start of the French Revolution in 1789 and the annexation of the Austrian Netherlands by the French Republic a couple of years later caused the production of expensive laces to slow and the banishing of lace from the fashionable male wardrobe.

Nineteenth-century mechanization led to lace overrunning everything. It colonized every part of women's attire. The full, crinoline-supported dresses and the numerous accessories fashion or etiquette demanded were ornamented with lacy flounces whose level of sophistication was determined by the husband's economic success. Remarkable masterpieces such as lace dresses attained unprecedented dimensions, effectively sounding the death knell for handmade lace as lace became the material for the entire dress, not just edgings or collars. Mechanization also reduced costs, encouraging the use of lace in the women's underwear sector.

None of this happened overnight, of course. It was a gradual process made possible in the first place by an adapted weaving machine devised by John Heathcoat in 1808. Between 1834 and 1841, the Leavers machine – which basically fitted a jacquard machine to Heathcoat's invention – was developed and perfected. From now on, mesh ground and patterns could be woven simultaneously. The Leavers machine produced mechanical lace, an openwork fabric combined with woven warp and weft threads.

The First World War put an end to the production of handmade lace in Belgium as well as its ostentatious application. But the fall in the popularity of lace was short-lived, as the end of the war saw a strong resurgence of mechanical lace, both for mourning wear and formal dresses. This was also the high point of metallic lace, worked into the stylized patterns prescribed by Art Deco.

In the 1930s, when social rules demanded a different outfit for each occasion, lace commanded pride of place as a choice for dresses worn to receptions, cocktail parties, gala dinners and other urbane events. Designers adored lace, for its delicacy and transparency highlighted the attractiveness of their creations. The trousseaus sold by the principle fashion houses (Lanvin, Premet, Poiret and so on) became so sophisticated that silk and lace nightwear – negligees, bed jackets, kimonos and so forth – was already being compared to evening wear.

After the Second World War and up until the mid-1960s, mechanical lace was further developed in all kinds of colour and pattern, sublimated in creations signed Dior, Balmain, Chanel or Balenciaga. Also, for the first time, nylon lace was integrated into undergarments helping to shape the female body.

Spring-Summer palette, handmade colour research using silk painting

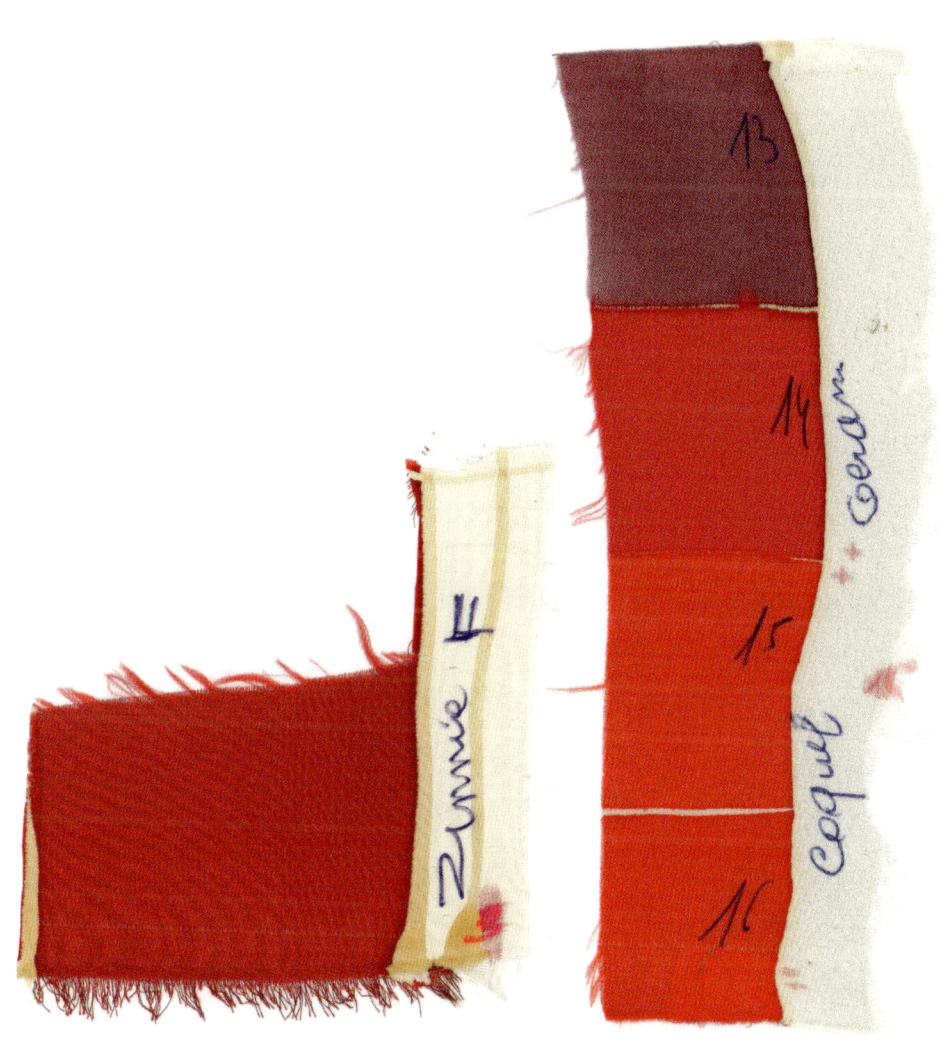

Coquelicot, handmade colour research using silk painting

Hand-painting on silk process, *Éphémère*,
Fall-Winter 2019 Evening, © Julien Leroy

Terre de Sienne, handmade colour research using silk painting

From the mid-1960s to the end of the 1970s, lace was out of fashion except in a very exclusive haute couture niche. A luxury fabric *par excellence*, it was deemed insufficiently modern by the young prêt-à-porter designers (and their clients) but it found a refuge in lingerie. Side by side with functional underwear, erotic lingerie developed steadily in the 1970s and especially in the 1980s, when the sexiness of lace was increasingly affirmed. The 1980s were characterized by a love of bombastic fashion, with many historic references, and lace as an element of sumptuous eveningwear made a comeback, specifically in collections by Christian Lacroix and Jean-Paul Gaultier. This period saw lingerie emerge from the private world of intimate apparel, as Madonna brandished it as a banner to vindicate girl power.

In the first two decades of the twenty-first century, lace was still used quite frequently for lingerie, both high-end and prêt-à-porter, as well as for couture designer clothes. By evolving from an ornamental detail to a fabric in its own right and subsequently an object of seduction as lingerie, lace has repeatedly reinvented itself. Carine Gilson keeps adding to the history of this creative adventure. On her watch, undergarments have become fully-fledged outerwear, to be worn during the day as well as for going out at night. Boundaries and codes are fading, transforming and renewing themselves.

CHANTILLY, CARINE GILSON'S FAVOURITE TYPE OF LACE

Although they look similar, handmade lace and machine lace are technically quite distinct. Gilson uses Chantilly lace. In 2019, Gilson joined forces with machine lace manufacturer Sophie Hallette to design and produce an exclusive type of lace that will represent her brand identity for the next ten years. This lace has been named Intemporelle.

Handmade Chantilly
Handmade Chantilly lace is made from silk (generally black silk yarn) using bobbins, on a mesh ground with two cross-twist threads forming a kind of triangle. It originated in Ile-de-France but really only began to be called Chantilly lace when it was no longer produced in the region. From 1840 onwards, most of it was made in Normandy (first Caen, then Bayeux) and in Belgium, in the area of Geraardsbergen (Grammont). This type of lace, very fashionable

Detail from a slip dress, *Rosa*, Fall-Winter 2017, © Stéphane Borremans

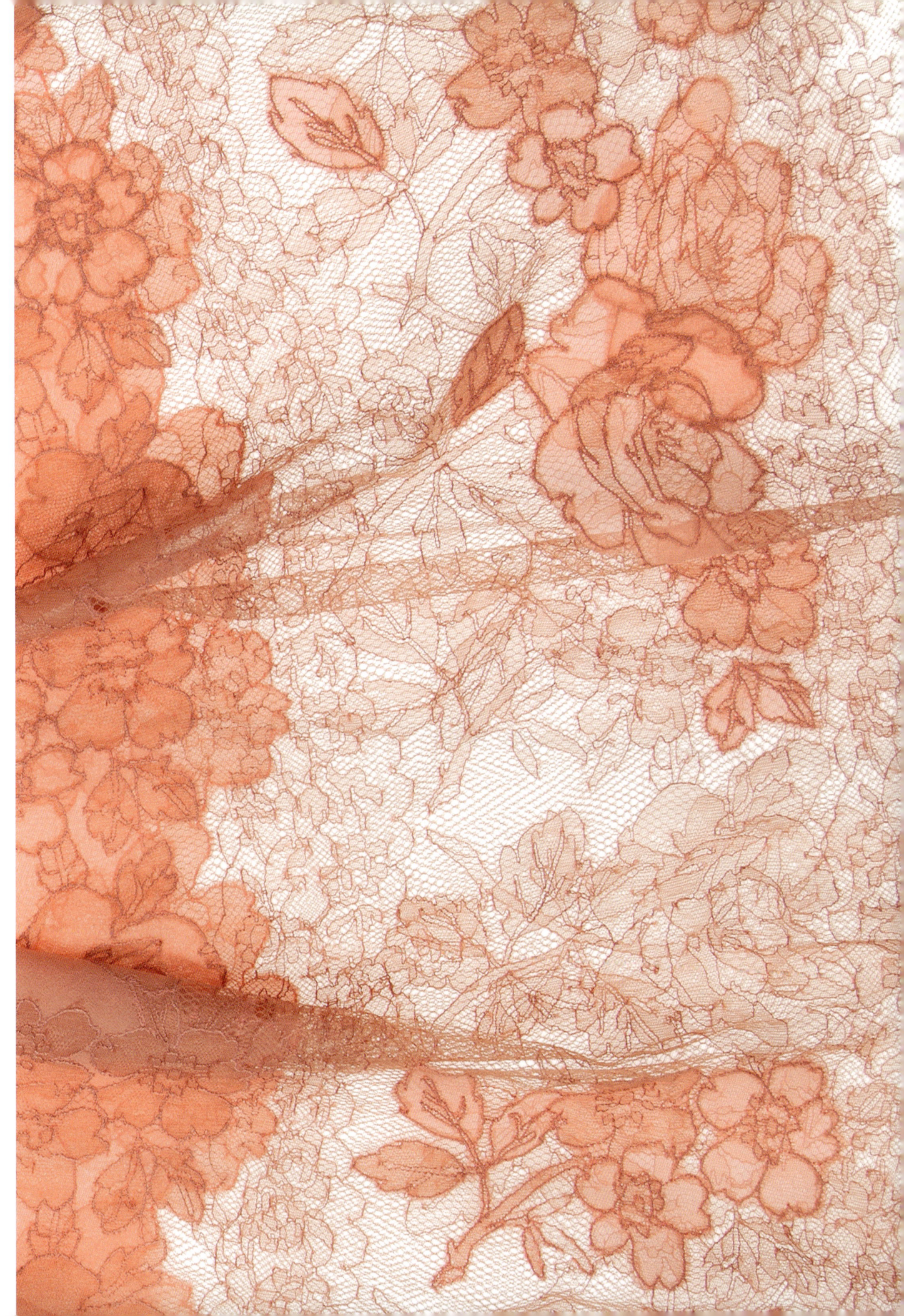

Work in progress during the creation of the exclusive Carine Gilson Intemporelle lace, 2019, © Julien Leroy

Original drawing by Carine Gilson, 2019

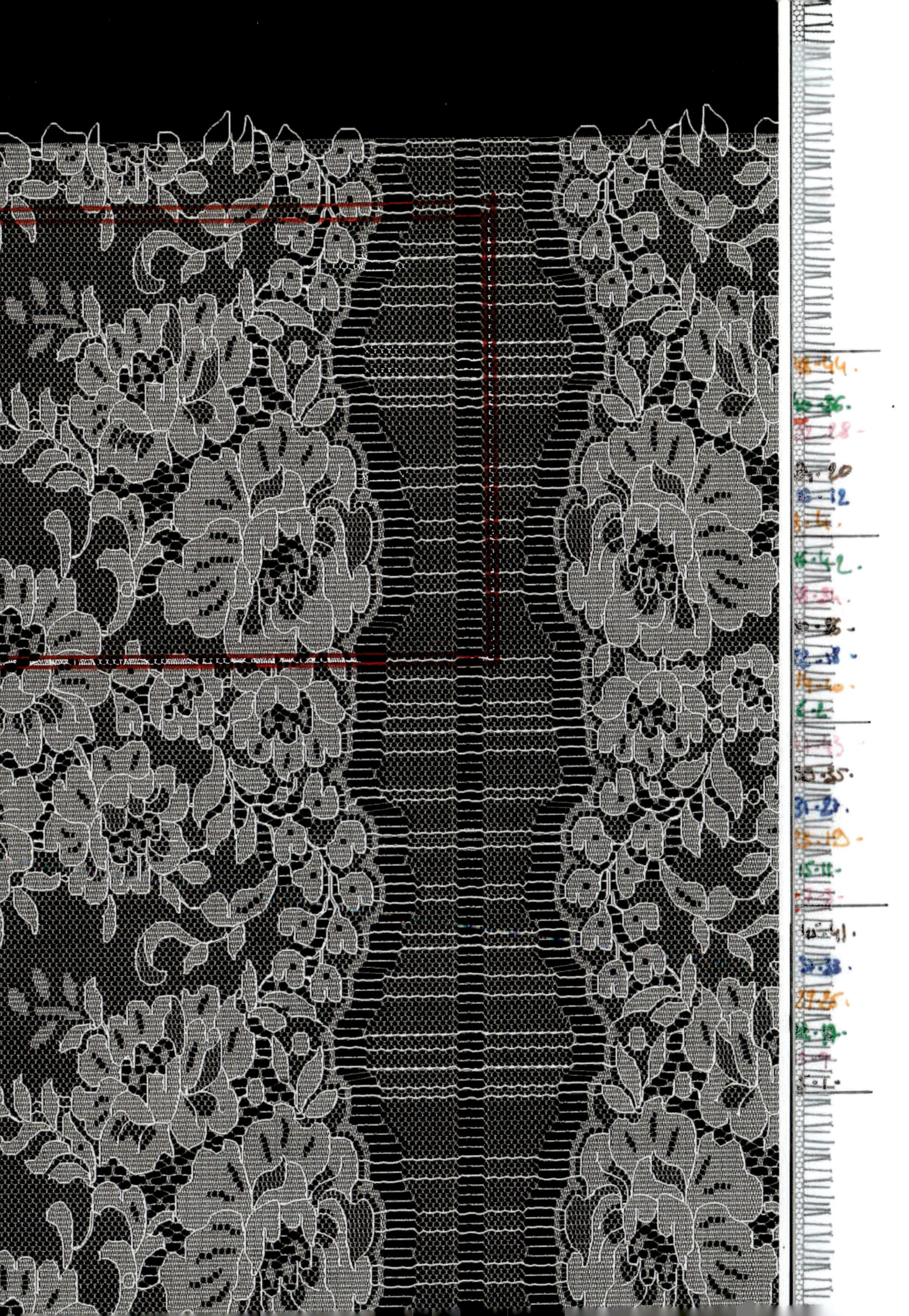

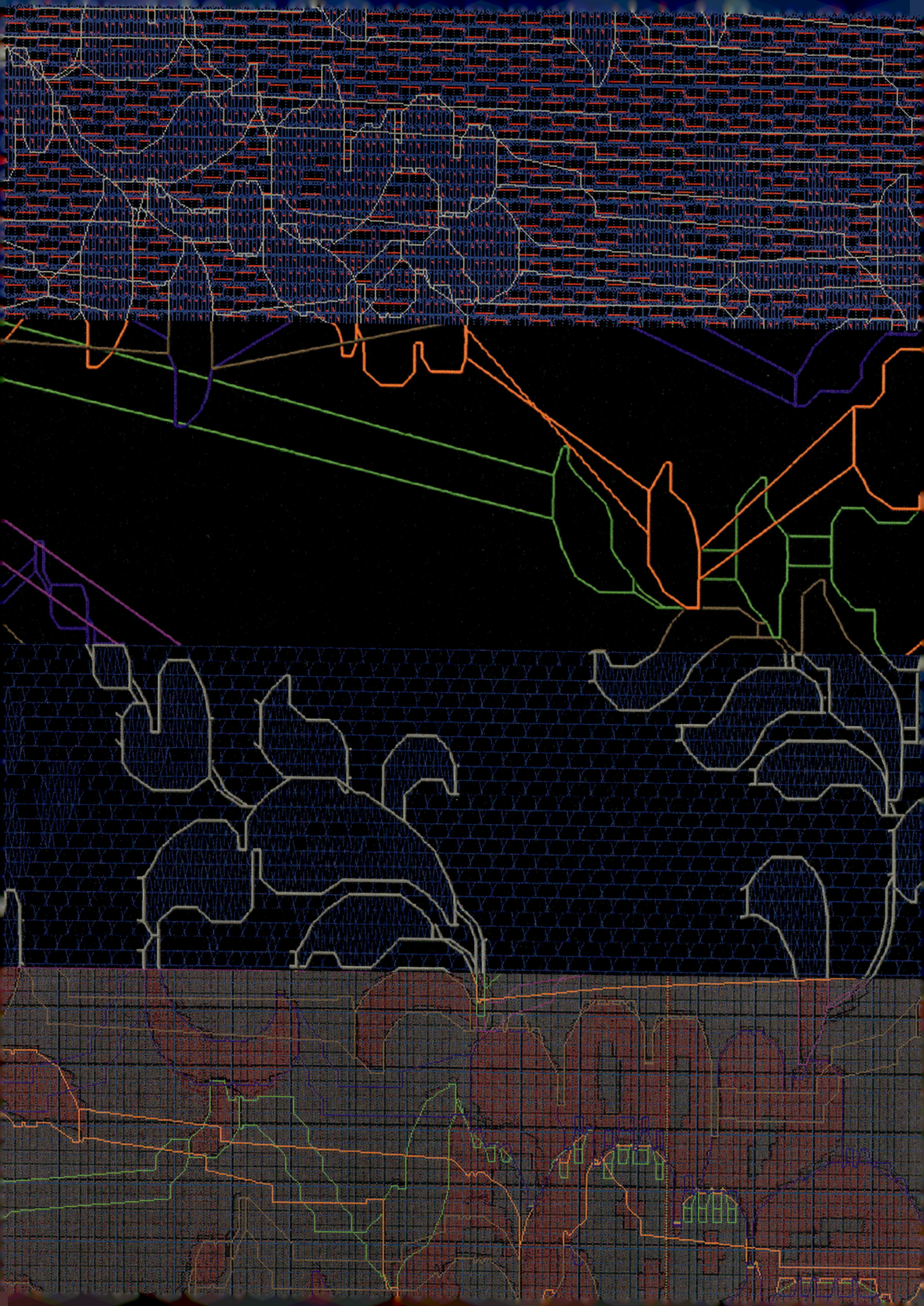

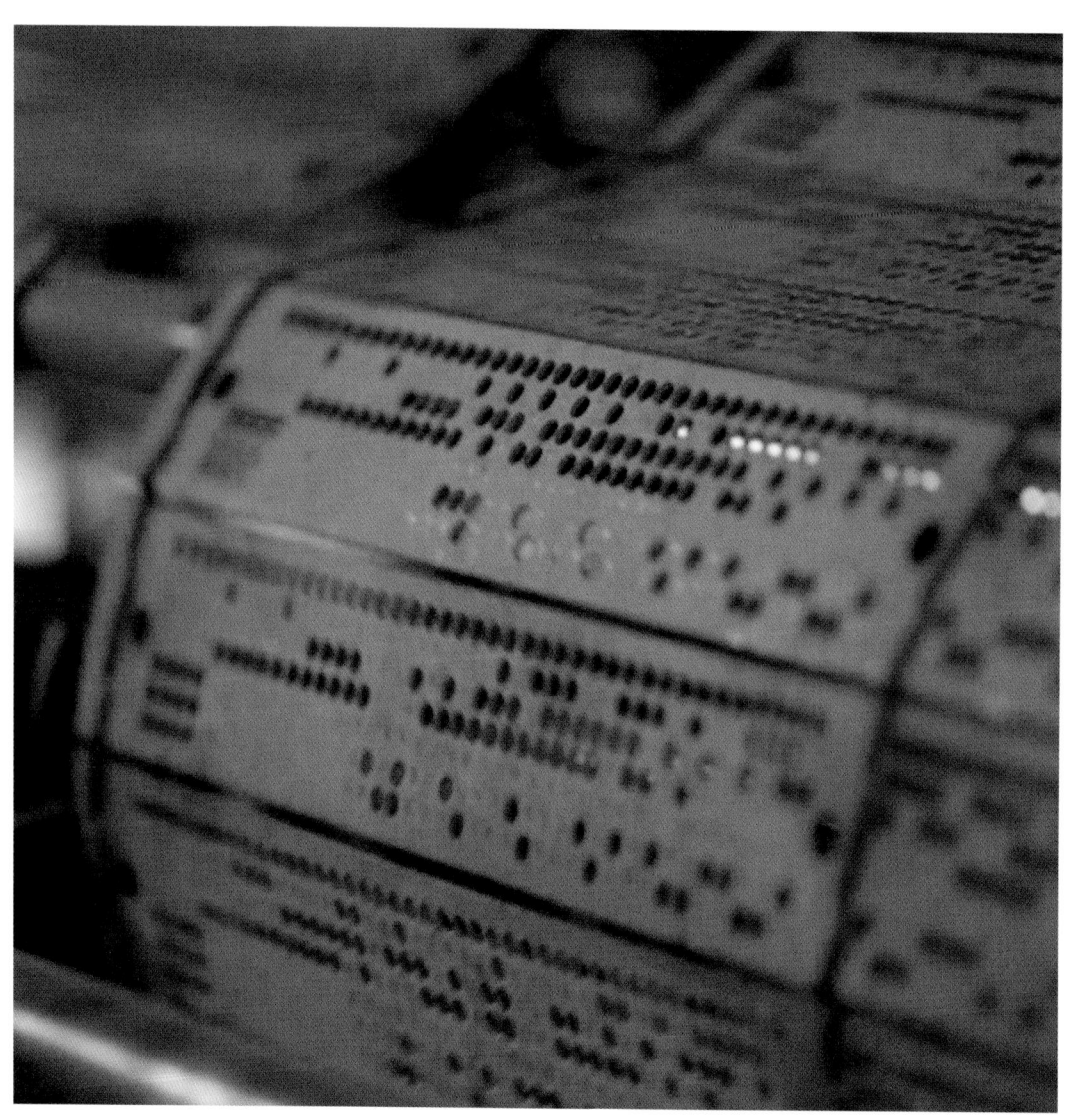

p. 70-71 preparation steps for the lace pattern mechanisation, 2019, © Sophie Hallette

p. 72-73 Technical images of the Intemporelle lace, 2019, © Sophie Hallette

Still image from the video *Mon coeur est de dentelle* from the *Beautiful Lace & Carine Gilson* exhibition at the Fashion & Lace Museum, July 10th 2019 to April 19th 2020, © Julie Pfleiderer and Luca Mattei for Carine Gilson

in the nineteenth century, was one of the first to be imitated mechanically – with great success.

Machine Lace Chantilly
Today, the term Chantilly designates a fine mechanical flowery lace of diaphanous beauty, close to the handmade variety. It can be made from the same materials and in every conceivable colour. For the thirtieth anniversary of her brand, Carine Gilson wanted to create her own timeless lace, for which she would develop the design. She shared her wish and decided to take up the challenge together with her favourite lace supplier, Maison Sophie Hallette.

A collaboration such as that between Carine Gilson and Sophie Hallette is unprecedented. It is prohibitively expensive to put a new design into production, and few manufacturers can make such an investment. But the long-standing cooperation, trust and loyalty between the Belgian stylist and the French manufacturer made the launching of Intemporelle possible.

From design drawing to finished product, via computer transcription and the weaving machine, the production of machine lace is a long process. From concept to delivery to the client, some twenty steps are required, which take up to six to eight weeks. The main steps in the creation of Intemporelle were these:

* A hand-drawn design by Carine Gilson. The design was conceived and created to provide endless possibilities for incrustation, and the borders, scalloped on each side, allow for playful mirroring.

* Sketches made by the creative team at Maison Sophie Hallette based on Gilson's hand-drawn design, which take into account the trajectories the threads will follow to produce the required patterns. It took three different sketches to arrive at the desired result. The final one is magnified about 400% on graph paper, to anticipate any deformations and breakages of the patterns in the production phase.

* The graph paper is scanned. This is where IT technology comes in, to register the passing of each thread and translate that into actions on the Leavers loom.*

* The threads are strung. A weaving machine may be strung with up to 11,000 warp threads (vertical) and 5,000 weft threads (horizontal).

* Production. The weaving process is constantly monitored: design, material, dimensions and potential faults are meticulously registered. Weaving a 40-centimetre strip of fabric takes twelve minutes.

* Output. When the lace comes off the loom it is off-white or white and may be slightly grubby from the greasy machinery. It must be washed and pre-formed before being dyed according to the client's wishes. The dyed strips of lace are cut as requested (straight or scalloped), checked again to detect and correct any remaining faults, and finally folded and packed, ready for shipping.

_{* The Leavers machine combines the bobbinet machine, invented in 1808, for weaving the mesh ground, and the jacquard machine, invented in 1801, for weaving patterns. It was developed from 1834 until 1841 and introduced in Calais and Caudry, where the lace industries developed that still exist today. The machine originally operated with a system of perforated cards to guide the passage of the threads. To produce a lace fabric, factory workers had to transfer the design onto punch cards and perforate them one by one. Since that era, technology has proved an enormous time-saver. Without it, perforating the cards would take three or four weeks longer.}

Leavers mechanical looms are enormous, weigh tons and make a deafening noise. The development of Leavers machines for the manufacture of lace marked the disappearance of nimble-fingered female lace-makers and their replacement by male factory workers. Though they now incorporate digital technology, those nineteenth-century machines are still in use today. Thus, with its 170 looms, Maison Sophie Hallette preserves the most important industrial heritage from Hauts de France.

With her Intemporelle lace pattern, Carine Gilson consolidates the identity of her brand.

Collection sketch by Carine Gilson, 1992

Preparatory sketches by Carine Gilson for *Flora*, Show Studio by Nick Knight, 2012

Courtesy Mme Figaro

+ grenière

Mon cœur
est
de dentelle

p. 84-85 Kirsten Dunst wearing Carine Gilson,
Tom Munro, Vanity Fair, © Conde Nast

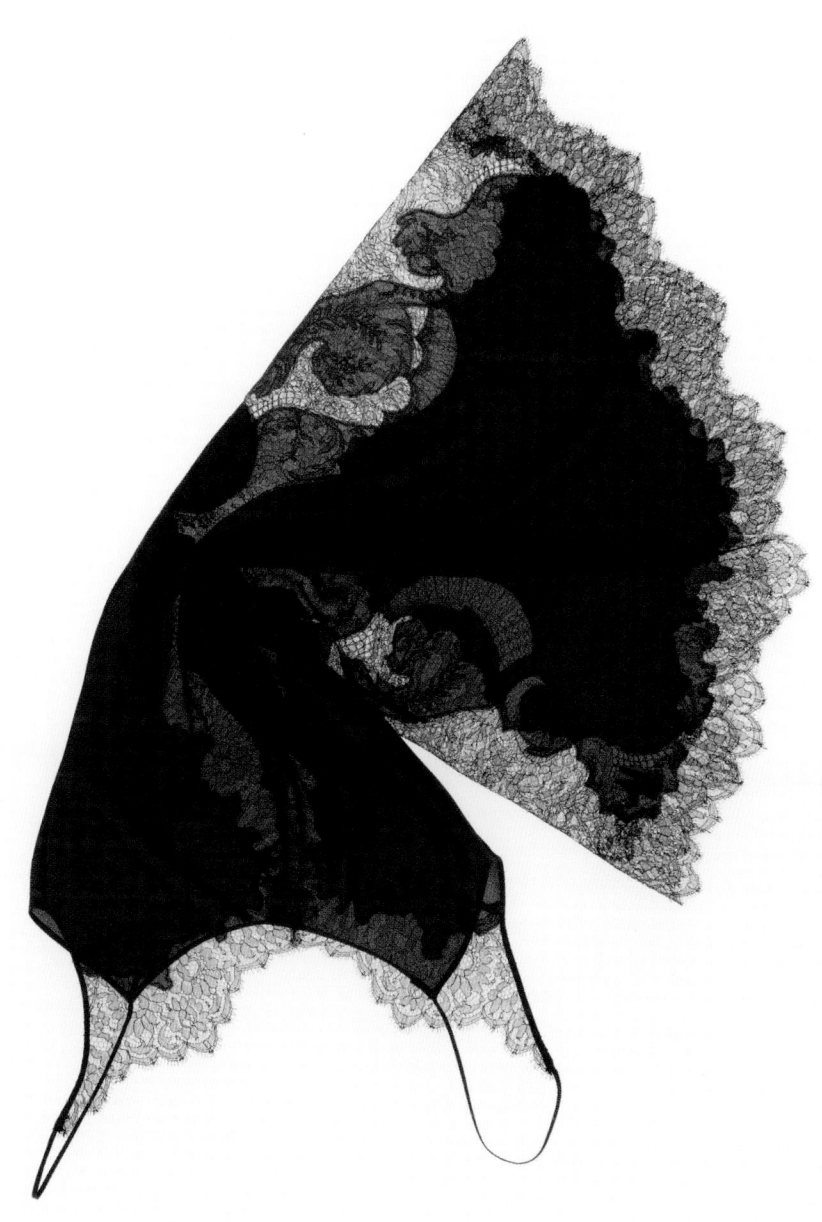

Still life, lace-incrusted silk slip dress, *Tubéreuse*,
Fall-Winter 2018, © Stéphane Borremans

Still life, lace-incrusted silk slip dress, *Tamara*, Fall-Winter 2012, © Xavier Harcq

Still life, lace-incrusted silk kimono, *Flora*, Spring-Summer 2019, © Stéphane Borremans

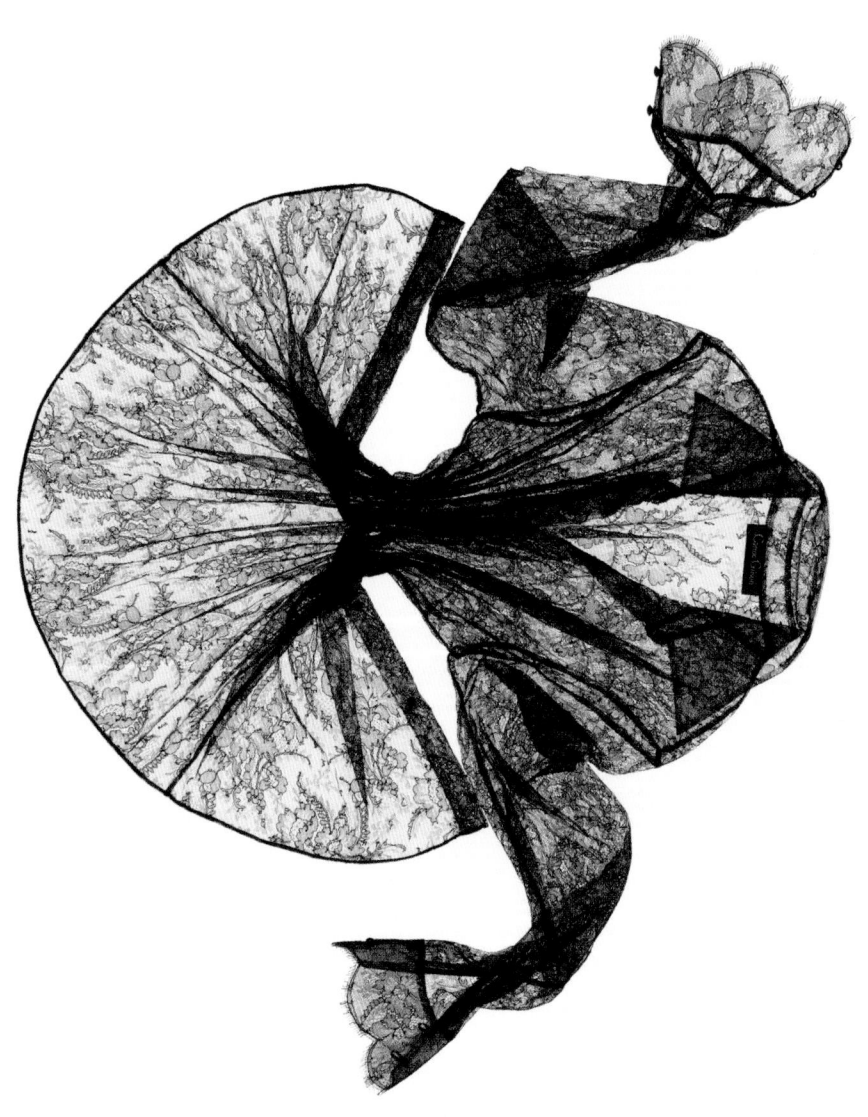

Still life, lace shirt, *Flora*, Spring-Summer 2019,
© Stéphane Borremans

Still life, lace and silk incrusted negligee, *Flora*,
Spring-Summer 2019, © Stéphane Borremans

Still life, lace-incrusted chiffon silk negligee, *Jardin de Paradis*, Fall-Winter 2015, © Stéphane Borremans

Still life, lace-incrusted silk slip dress, *Alba*, Spring-Summer 2015, © Stéphane Borremans

MON COEUR EST FAIT DE DENTELLE

Karen Van Godtsenhoven

In the quiet recess of her atelier, Carine Gilson communes with her muse, lace, by making still life photographs that capture her creations like rare flowers or birds of paradise in flight. These feather-light, diaphanous pieces in silk and lace are painstakingly arranged and rearranged (perhaps as many as fifty times), folded, draped and fanned out on top of a light source. Like a Rorschach inkblot, the emerging shapes reveal the veiled mysteries hidden in their maker's mind. The symbiosis of lace and silk becomes a work of art, a chiaroscuro painting of fleeting beauty, captured by lightning.

In *The Painter of Modern Life*, Charles Baudelaire observes that it is not the naked body one desires, but the clothed body, the silhouette clad in silk, velvet and lace: just as in his memories of childhood, where the fabrics of his mother's clothes would evoke her embrace, he later delights in the sight of his mistress attired in her finery, which he sees as an indivisible unity of body and cloth. In Gilson's images the gaze is directed by the fabric, the residuum not the body. The body has stepped out of or is yet to be enveloped in the lace. Nonetheless, our eye is mesmerized, held in thrall by the suggestion of affection and desire.

Naturally introverted, Gilson has been making these images ever since she began to work with lace. The process gives her a way of quietly speaking and travelling with her own work; it's the purest way for her to express herself, to redirect her creative energy into her own work, to look at it with new eyes. As keeper of the flame or patient alchemist, Gilson brings the fabrics to life, draping and unfolding them into shapes resembling floral arabesques. The sculpted three-dimensional fabric is arrested in a flat image that seems to quiver with motion: a baroque reverie of ornament, light and movement. The body is absent yet implicit, as the movement of the fabrics seems to hold the curves and twists of a body in

Still life, lace-incrusted silk scarf-top, *Cérès*, Pre-Fall-Winter 2016, © Stéphane Borremans

Still life, lace-incrusted pleated silk slip dress, *Art Nouveau*, Fall-Winter 2005, © Stéphane Borremans

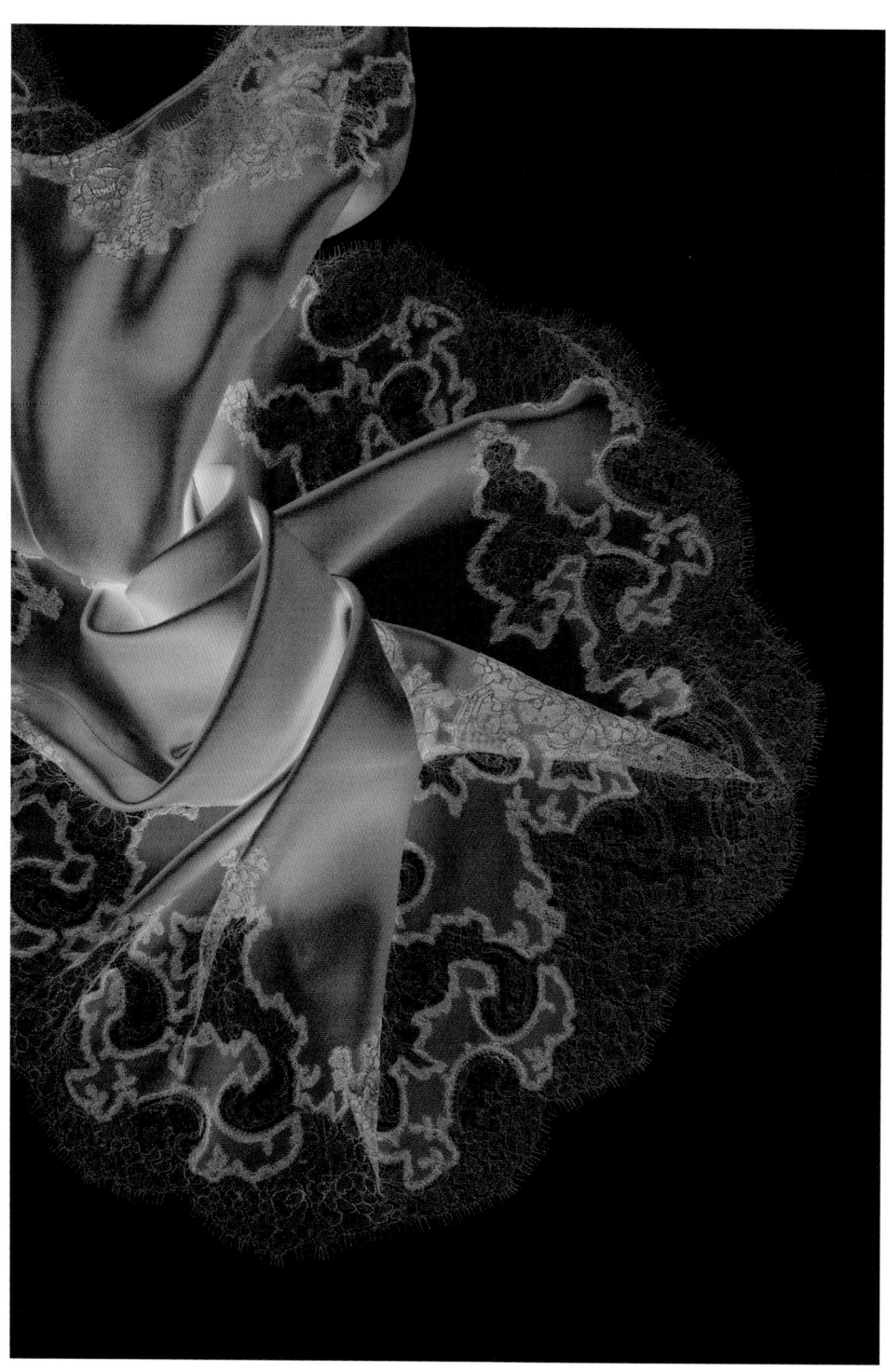

Still life, lace-incrusted silk slip dress, *l'Envol*, Fall-Winter 2019, © Stéphane Borremans

Still life, lace incrusted silk slip dress, *Collection Venise*, Fall-Winter 2008, © Stéphane Borremans

movement, in balletic flight, perhaps in Stravinsky's *Firebird*, composed for Diaghilev's Ballets Russes, choreographed by Michel Fokine. The lavish orientalist balls hosted by Paul Poiret, such as the 'Thousand-and-Second Night', can be glimpsed through the swirling gestures of the shimmering silk and lace. Even though Gilson calls her arrangements 'still lifes', there is music to be heard in these arrangements, lively dances and soft lullabies.

Gilson discovers these images by seeing things in her own work which other people cannot. It is a form of the sublime, as precious as a butterfly's wing. Some still lifes recall images of nineteenth-century botanical cabinets, other transport the eye to the sweeping gestures of Japanese calligraphy or contemporary abstract art. The rhythmic, scrolling and interlacing lines of the lace evoke the architecture of the Middle East, yet one can also see the skeletal imprints of openwork spires of Gothic cathedrals in the incrusted lacework. As testimonies of passion and precision, the still lifes invite the eye into a place beyond the frame, a secret garden of dreams and inspiration.

p. 101-102 Still life, Chantilly shawl, circa 1900 (Silk thread, motifs and background created on bobbins using the continuous thread technique. 310 cm x 145 cm.)
Fashion and Lace Museum, inv. D77.01.02. Lace shawl, Fashion and Lace Museum archive, Brussels, © Stéphane Borremans

p. 103 Still life, Ruffle with Brussels lace application on mechanised tulle. 1860-1870.
Linen and cotton threads, patterns created with bobbin and needle on mechanised tulle. 35 cm x 625 cm.
This item belonged to 'Sisi', Empress Elisabeth of Austria (1837-1898), and comes from a famous lace manufacturer, the Maison Verdé-Delisle Frères & Cie (Compagnie des Indes), located in Paris and Brussels.
Fashion and Lace Museum, inv. D88.46.01., Fashion and Lace Museum archive, Brussels © Stéphane Borremans

III

ATELIER

Detail from a kimono, *Flora*, Spring-Summer 2019,
© Stéphane Borremans

Image from the *Beautiful Lace & Carine Gilson* exhibition at the Fashion & Lace Museum, July 10th 2019 to April 19th 2020, © JPohl

Detail from the *Beautiful Lace & Carine Gilson* exhibition at the Fashion & Lace Museum, July 10th 2019 to April 19th 2020, © Julien Leroy

4m80
silk is needed to make a long kimono

484 pins
are stitchted on by hand, one by one,
to place the lace on an underdress

18 000m
lace flowers are inlaid every year

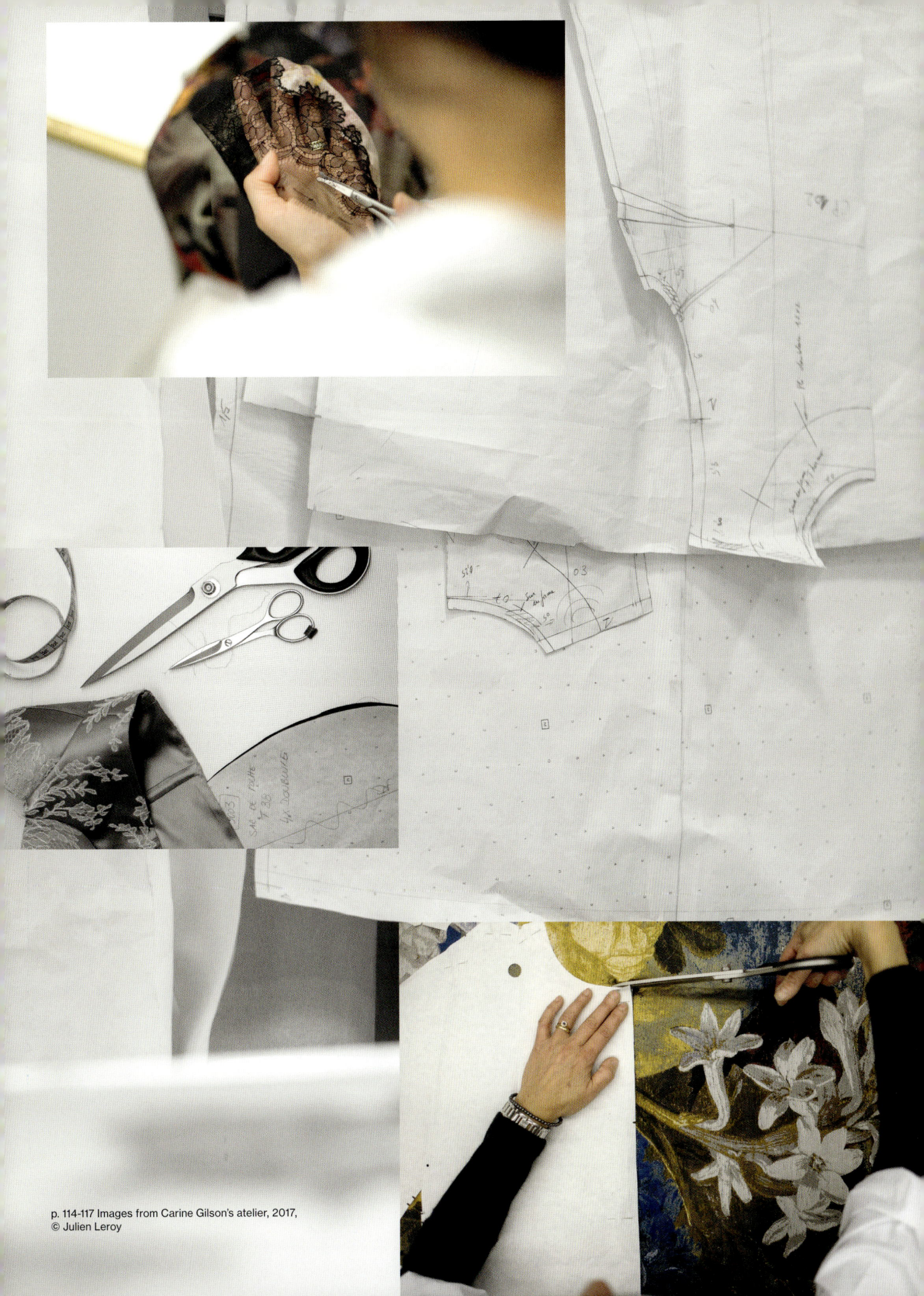

p. 114-117 Images from Carine Gilson's atelier, 2017,
© Julien Leroy

Printed long kimono from the *Beautiful Lace & Carine Gilson* exhibition at the Fashion & Lace Museum, July 10th 2019 to April 19th 2020, *Tubéreuse*, Fall-Winter 2018, © Stéphane Borremans

Image from the *Beautiful Lace & Carine Gilson* exhibition at the Fashion & Lace Museum, July 10th 2019 to April 19th 2020, © Stéphane Borremans

'LACE-INCRUSTED SILK IS MY HANDWRITING. I LIKE TO RE-DRAW IT, AS IF I WAS WRITING WITH A PEN.'

Caroline Esgain

While preparing for the exhibition of her work at the Fashion & Lace Museum in Brussels, Carine Gilson was allowed to roam the museum's storage spaces and explore the lace fabrics held in its collections. Very exceptionally she was permitted to handle and examine its old handmade pieces. Some of these struck her as perfect exhibition material, such as the wonderful flounces in Brussels application on mechanical tulle that once belonged to Empress Elisabeth of Austria or 'Sisi' as she was affectionately known (1860-1870). What do these pieces from various origins have in common? The beauty of their design. The abundance, delicacy, luxuriousness, refinement and evanescence of nature, which are such an inspiration to Carine Gilson, are the qualities that strike her in lace motifs, which she re-draws onto silk fabrics by means of the incrustation technique.

Lace incrustation is central to her work but there is another, less prominent feature that is also a major aspect of her identity, that being her creation of exclusive prints on silk fabric. From the very start, Gilson used the finest silks and an exclusive palette for her collections. Since 2015, her quest for preciousness has also been reflected in her designs for printed silk fabrics, which make the silk-lace dialogue complete. Silk, lace and print come together to create a trilogy that is renewed with every collection theme. *Jardin de Paradis* (2015-2016), *Jardin d'Eden* (2015), *Lost in Wonderland* (2016-2017), *Sketch of Paradise* (2018) and *Les Tubéreuses* (2018-2019) are just some of the prints in which Gilson expresses her view of the Garden of Eden.

In March 2019, while photographing a Chantilly lace shawl in the museum's collection as part of her 'still life' process, Gilson was struck by the beauty of its motifs and the seductiveness of the stylized flowers. It was love at first sight, a revelation. The motifs in the antique lace seemed to her like a new garden to wander in and explore, piece by piece. Despite looming deadlines, she decided to turn this newly discovered motif into the centrepiece of her forthcoming collection and a major theme of the

Detail from a kimono, silk screen, Garden of Lace Cruise 2020, © Stéphane Borremans

Silk screen frames, © Maison Carine Gilson

Silk screen frame, detail, © Maison Carine Gilson

Beautiful Lace exhibition.

She completely redrafted the layout of the shawl's motifs on paper. Four compositions were transferred onto silkscreen frames and printed on silk fabrics. In fact, at that point Gilson was once again working with the techniques she had embraced at the start of her career. Clearly, crafting by hand and the feelings and emotions that evokes in her were still very dear to her heart. This is how the *Garden of Lace* came about.

At that stage, the motif was still monochrome, as in the undyed test specimen displayed in the first showcase in the *Beautiful Lace & Carine Gilson* exhibition: a negligee in incrusted silk and organza print in a decor of assorted silk *charmeuse*.

This sums up the new working method Gilson has developed specifically to deal with antique lace that inspires her but cannot be incrusted or cut up. In a very real sense she is re-drawing the lace; it becomes the ink in her pen. The sophisticated vegetal motifs on Sisi's flounces will be the designer's next inspiration. But that is another chapter, still to be written…

Detail of hand-pleated lace, *Éphémère*, Fall-Winter 2019 Evening, © Maison Carine Gilson

Detail of hand-pleated lace process, *Éphémère*, Fall-Winter 2019 Evening, © Maison Carine Gilson

p. 132-133 Image from the *Beautiful Lace & Carine Gilson* exhibition at the Fashion & Lace Museum, July 10th 2019 to April 19th 2020, © detiffe.com

THE TROUSSEAU

Caroline Esgain & Catherine Gauthier

A trousseau is, or at least was until the mid-twentieth century, the complete set of linen and garments a girl would gather in preparation for her impending marriage. Underwear and everyday clothes were hand-made with utmost care and embroidered with the bride's initials. Needlework and housekeeping were taught to every girl, no matter her social background. Though some made their own trousseaus, or at least embroidered their linens with their own monogram, wealthier girls commissioned theirs from dressmakers who delivered made-to-measure sets. When haute couture came into existence, designers would propose an entire trousseau, a complete range of lingerie and loungewear – negligees, peignoirs, underdresses, slips, bed jackets and dressing gowns. The quality and quantity of the pieces were commensurate with the fiancée's wealth. Magazines from the 1920s and 1930s presented creations by renowned fashion houses (Lanvin, Poiret, etc.) that displayed a sophistication and preciousness equal to that of their evening gowns. Though this tradition has fallen out of use, the concept of refined, sophisticated loungewear seems to have reappeared, at least the premium category desired by Maison Gilson's clientele.

For her international clients, Carine Gilson assembles tailor-made trousseaus consisting of up to 150 items. Commissions of this kind invariably lead to a close relationship between designer and client. Rather than sending an assistant or seamstress, Gilson herself will propose various models to the client, lending her advice and taking all the measurements. New and unique pieces may be created for the occasion, but more often than not, clients choose customized versions of existing models.

New-York show, 2011, © Stéphane Borremans

p. 138-139 Behind the scene of the atelier and backstage of the 25th anniversary show, © Philippe Graton

Flowers setting by Thierry Boutemy, backstage of the 25th anniversary show, © Philippe Graton

p. 142-143 Still image from the video of the 25th anniversary show, 2015, © Stéphane Borremans

VI

A GARDEN OF HER OWN

Hummingbird and Passion Flowers, ca 1875-85,
Martin Johnson Heade

Jacquard tapestry representing *La Tubéreuse Casée*, Frans Van Dael © Métaphores

Bas Meeuws (Netherlands, 1974), *Tulip Book (#05)*, 2012, C-Print on dibond behind acrylic, © Bas Meeuws/ courtesy of Per van der Horst Gallery

p. 149-151 25th anniversary campaign, *Jardin de Paradis*, Fall-Winter 2015, © Stéphane Borremans, model Kim Peers

A GARDEN OF HER OWN: THIRTY YEARS OF INSPIRATION IN THE WORK OF CARINE GILSON

Karen Van Godtsenhoven

Growing steadily like a vine that weaves across a wall and meets its own stems again, over the course of thirty years, the current of inspiration that runs through Carine Gilson's work has been augmented, extended, repeated and refined. At the heart of her own mental Garden of Eden is her muse – lace. It acts as a sensual connective tissue to the skin, whispering to the body and drawing motifs on it as it plays with the light. The lace, whether handmade and cream-colored or machine-made and black, un-borders the silk. Rather than enclosing it, it creates a permeable border between the body and the light and the air that surrounds it. In perfect harmony with the finest silk, lace makes the wearer aware of her body's sensation of self, adorning her with beauty, self-confidence and care. The wearer is the Carine Gilson woman, dreamy and mysterious, connected to the designer but not the same, a constantly changing and growing personality who wanders around her private Garden of Eden.

This is the woman, standing at the centre of her universe, her own muse, who pre-eminently appreciates the sensual pleasures provided by the CG negligees, kimonos, caracos and *combinaisons* or slip dresses. Thus, the dual motivating forces of inspiration at the heart of the label – the material lace and the Carine Gilson woman – create the tension that drives artistic creation: the mental strength and ultra-feminine aura of the wearer, be she *garçonne* or curvaceous, is in contrast with the fragility of the lace. Whatever her age, the woman Gilson envisions always has a strong sense of self and purpose. She is not the object to be adorned but the subject living in the silk and lace. The delicate flowers of the lace accompany a strong woman directing her own gaze and desire. The different floral patterns, petals, curls, vines and leaves represent a plethora of characters, which Gilson weaves into the patchwork of the Carine Gilson woman who surrounds herself with beauty. She is attentive to detail and obsessed by precision, which she enjoys in private like

Untitled, Karl Blossfeldt

Venise lace
Fern, Karl Blossfeldt

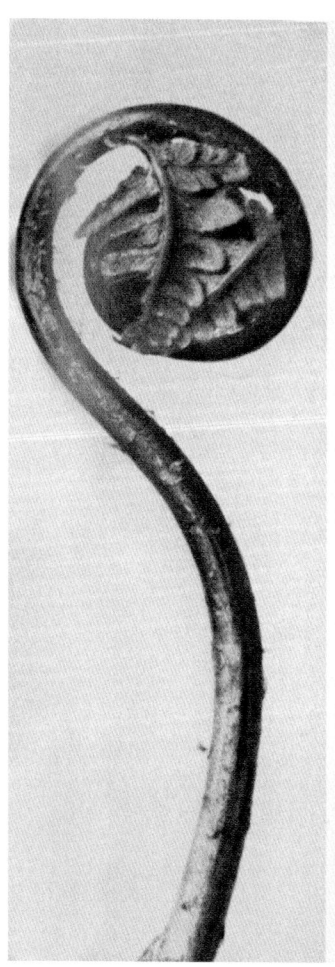
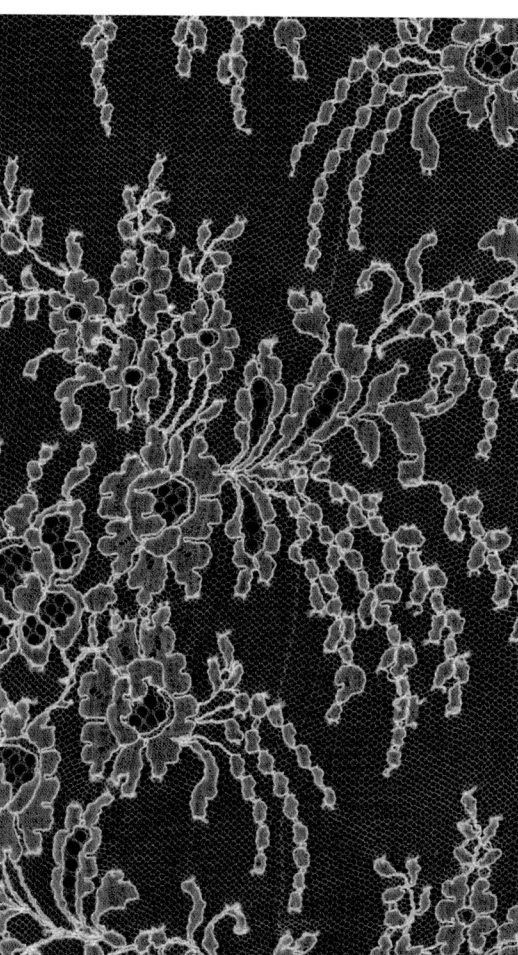

Heliotrope, Karl Blossfeldt

Florence lace
Blueberry, Karl Blossfeldt

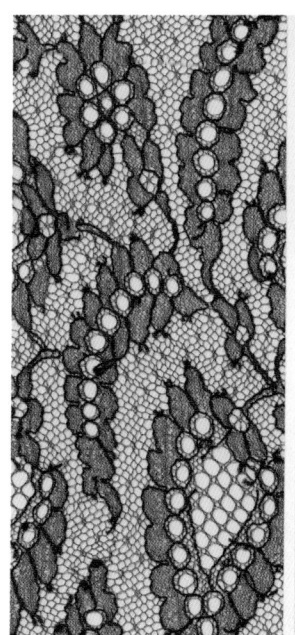

the old-school dandy. The smallest aesthetic pleasures can evoke heartfelt emotions. With a Baudelairean perception of surrender to the senses and an appreciation of ephemeral beauty, she enjoys what other people do not see, in her own secret Garden of Eden, a lush and sensuous yet orderly land.

Delving deep into the aesthetic codes and early seedlings of inspiration in Gilson's work we find threads of Japonism, Orientalism, Art Nouveau and Art Deco, which with time, patience and enduring perfectionism have all become an ingrained part of her creative signature. The sinuous florals and swirling sensuality of Art Nouveau merge into the graphic contrast and symmetrical lines of Art Deco; in Gilson's world, different influences are in harmonious equipoise. Her motto, that 'Everything is a paradox', causes her to embrace and combine different ideas and aesthetics into an essence that bears enough newness to surprise. These days, Gilson's creative flow has become so intuitive, her signature so mature, that she can look inside and listen to the material in order to tell her story.

Her early collections focused on single narrative themes such as the Ballets Russes (1909-1929), the Modernist and abstract Orientalist spectacles by Sergei Diaghilev, for which Gabrielle Chanel and Léon Bakst created the costumes while the colourful sets were designed by such illustrious names as Pablo Picasso and Henri Matisse. The modernism and exoticism of the Ballets Russes gave the body more freedom than classical ballet: it is that feeling of freedom of movement and weightlessness that is still part of Gilson's signature.

The work of Polish Art Deco artist Tamara de Lempicka is another early reference for Gilson: the languorous women in her paintings, the way she has rendered their lingering gazes, the decadent atmosphere, the Cubist effects of light on the draped silk, changing its tone. More Orientalist inspiration in Gilson's early work comes from the masquerade balls hosted by fashion designer Paul Poiret, who took silhouettes and shapes from the Middle East and Far East (such as harem trousers and kimono-type coats) and here in the West transformed them into luxurious evening wear – long loose garments that liberated women from the corset. The sensual abundance, the luxurious excess of the fabrics and the resplendent finery, combined with the rich imagination at the heart of these

Farm garden with Sunflowers, 1907, Gustav Klimt,
© Belvedere, Vienna, photo Johannes Stoll

creations, inspired Gilson's early work and her quest for the finest silks and lace, as well as her interpretation of the kimono as a piece of sumptuous evening wear or underwear.

More Orientalist influences appear in Gilson's work in the form of chinoiserie (the incrustation of lace and the refined floral patterns) and the aesthetic of Japonism, the late-nineteenth- and early-twentieth-century art movement by which the West appropriated an idealized notion of Japan. Japonism, as a modern, Western lens for Japanese arts, provided an aesthetic that influenced the Impressionists and a lot of modern architecture and design schools such as Art Nouveau and Art Deco, as well as Gustav Klimt, whose stylized portraits and colourful, enigmatic compositions are beloved by Gilson. Japonism conveys a highly subjective and intuitive notion of a Japan that is enthralling, enchanted and mysterious, characterized by the idea of the perfect brushstroke, a sophisticated artistry steeped in profound respect for tradition and the nature of a material. The pure T-shape of the kimono is the basis for many of Gilson's creations, for it provides the perfect freedom, comfort and aesthetic for the delicate lace incrustation that echoes the effects of mother of pearl cherry blossom motifs found on dark lacquerware or Japanese screens. Its wide butterfly silk sleeves, often in a half-tone colour inspired by the lush fauna and flora of exotic gardens, exude an avian feeling of lightness and flight. When Gilson works on kimonos, the placement of the lace design on the kimono is key for the composition. Evoking the beauty of the Japanese *ukiyo-e* woodblock prints, she creates silk camisoles with a low-cut back, echoing the importance of the graceful line of the back in Japanese arts. An *obi* belt in silk crepe holds a hand-folded train in lace, cascading down the back in a blend of Eastern lines and Western materials, in an eternal pursuit of beauty.

In *The Painter of Modern Life* (1863), the nineteenth century poet Charles Baudelaire posited a definition of beauty that encompassed two notions, one related to the classical, eternal and immutable in art and one to the inconstant, ephemeral and fugitive in art, which he called the modern sensibility. The successful artist knows how to combine the skills of the old masters in order to capture contemporary life: similarly, in her atelier, Gilson uses the craftsmanship and know-how of past couturiers in order to create something new.

The course of her own life and artistic path fuel her creative engine, too. In many ways her own muse, she is also her own master and mentor, as she moves in a matriarchal universe, emboldened by the pioneering spirit of the early female couturiers such as Madeleine,

The Large-Flowering Sensitive Plant from the *Temple of Flora*, 1807, Robert John Thornton

Phacelea Tanacetifolia, 1900-25, Karl Blossfeldt

Bird of Paradise, courtesy of Harold F. Sherwood

Geishas from *The Japs at Home*, published by Ward and Co., 1895, The British Library

Incrusted long kimono, *l'Envol*, Fall-Winter 2019, © Maison Carine Gilson

Incrusted long kimono, *Jardin d'Eden*, Spring-Summer 2016, © Maison Carine Gilson

170 *Orientalisme* campaign, Spring-Summer 1996,
© Stéphane Borremans, model Germaine

Vionnet, Mme Grès, Jeanne Lanvin and Gabrielle Chanel, who – each in her own way – emancipated and elevated the tradition of female craftsmanship in the fashion industry not only into a form of applied art but also into a highly successful business. The *savoir-faire* of their collaborative practice (with a system of premières, the most important right hand to the designer) inspires Gilson's own work in her atelier.

The artistry and scientific precision of Madeleine Vionnet inspired Gilson so much that she worked on small dolls for a while, mirroring the practice of her predecessor, who famously worked on three-quarter-scale dolls to try out experimental designs that were cut on the bias – diagonal to the fabric's weave – thus creating a sort of body-hugging, pyjama-like silk cocoon. Vionnet's eveningwear liberated the body from its constraining corseted carapace and enveloped it in a gentle embrace. Her singular, non-seasonal

Louise Brooks in Ziegfeld Follie's

artistic stance and creative legacy have been a lifelong inspiration for Gilson, teaching her first and foremost that with sheer mental strength and a will to succeed, anything was possible. If women could successfully run fashion houses in the interwar period, young Carine could also start her own label more than half a century later. Gilson taught herself the basics of the bias cut from Betty Kirke's influential book on the life and work of Madeleine Vionnet, which elucidates the patterns and techniques – not unlike engineering – of the legendary couturier. This monumental volume is on many a designer's bookshelf, including Gilson's: after all these years she has absorbed the techniques so much she has made them her own. More than any technique, however, it is the vision of Vionnet and Madame Grès and the willpower, not to say sheer stubbornness, of Gabrielle Chanel that have inspired Gilson's mental force, for they demonstrated to her that 'one can reach the goal by doing everything possible in order to arrive at the port where your ship wants to lay its anchor.'

After years of fine-tuning and immersing herself in diverse yet key sources of inspiration ranging from the Ballets Russes and Japonism to Art Deco and Art Nouveau, Gilson's approach is more like that of a singer who intuitively picks and mixes melodies from a well-known repertoire. She re-arranges, modulates and rewrites the silhouettes into a new collection, which, once completed, she finds it hard to look at again. For her 2019 retrospective *Garden of Lace* in the Fashion & Lace Museum in Brussels, however, she had no choice but to go into her archives and look at her early work, which pulled her in deeper to take a second look and rework early collections. In her own hands and eyes, she transformed some of the pieces she made as a young woman into a contemporary vision, scrutinizing details in which she can lose herself, recomposing the various layers and techniques accumulated over the years. It's normal for fashion designers to feel ambivalent about their early work, given that they are invariably looking forwards rather than back. In the case of Carine Gilson – who is her own harshest critic – that process became an intense yet exhilarating experience.

Today, Gilson's spirit is still imbued with the themes that preoccupied her in the beginning, the vine of inspiration still runs through her work, which has the Garden of Eden of lace and the idea of the private mental boudoir at its heart. Her collections have matured and become purer, more self-aware, instinctual rather than narrative.

p. 174-175 Contact sheet from the *Orientalisme* collection, Spring-Summer 1996, © Stéphane Borremans, model Germaine

Danseuse de profil, à genoux, Prélude à l'après-midi d'un faune, 1914, Baron Adolf de Meyer, © Musée d'Orsay, Paris

Costume for Vaslav Nijinsky as the Faun, 1935-37,
Leon Bakst, © Wadsworth Atheneum Museum of Art

Costume of Cleopatra for Ida Rubinstain, 1909,
Leon Bakst, © Lobanov-Rostovsky Collection

Russian Ballets, Spring-Summer 1997,
© Stéphane Borremans, model Milou

Tamara Karsavina as the firebird in *The Firebird*, London, 1911, © Curatorial Assistance Inc./E. O. Hoppé Estate Collection

Likewise, the logo of the brand has evolved from the birds of paradise drawing into an orientalist, calligraphic image with abstract avian and floral qualities, uniting the core sensibilities of Art Deco, preciosity and Japonism at the heart of the Carine Gilson aesthetic. The exuberant, wing-like curls represent the future, the departure of a new flight.

It has always been so with me from my boyhood. There is not a single colour hidden away in the chalice of a flower, or the curve of a shell, to which, by some subtle sympathy with the very soul of things, my nature does not answer.

Oscar Wilde, *De Profundis*, 1905

CARINE GILSON IN FIVE POINTS

1989-1992: Shortly after she left from the Royal Academy of Fine Arts in Antwerp, Carine Gilson falls in love with the authentic atmosphere at Maille France, a Brussels manufacturer that has been producing lingerie since 1928. She buys the business and, while continuing to produce lingerie bearing the Maille France name, completes her apprenticeship as an expert in lace incrustation on silk.

1992-1998: Maille France becomes Vanités by Maille France in 1994, then Vanités – Exclusive collection by C. Gilson in 1996. Encouraged by this experience, Carine Gilson produces and develops her first lingerie collections, which soon gain international success thanks to their distribution in luxury boutiques (London, Paris, New York and the Middle East).

1998-2005: The label C. Gilson – Couture Lingerie turns its mastery of the incrustation of lace on silk, which the fashion house has elevated to a high level of artistic craftsmanship, into a trademark. Carine Gilson opens several additional boutiques, including, in 2005, one in Paris, where she develops the concept of the Garden of Eden, a theme that repeatedly recurs in her exclusive prints.

2005-2018: Carine Gilson – Couture Lingerie. To mark the twentieth anniversary of her brand, in 2009, Carine Gilson opens a boutique in Rue Antoine Dansaert in Brussels, and a few months later presents an unprecedented show in New York. Her creations are worn by celebrities and each new collection causes a stir. As of 2016, the range of garments presented by the brand is expanded with evening wear that seems to have escaped from the more intimate section of the wardrobe.

2018-2019: Maison Carine Gilson. The designer moves her Brussels boutique in Rue Antoine Dansaert to Boulevard de Waterloo, to a new showcase conceived in collaboration with the design studio david/nicolas. To mark the thirtieth anniversary of her brand, Carine Gilson teams up with lace manufacturer Sophie Hallette to create an exclusive lace that will become the brand's identity for her timeless signature designs.

SELECT BIBLIOGRAPHY

Martine Bruggeman, *L'Europe de la dentelle. Un aperçu historique depuis les origines de la dentelle jusqu'à l'entre-deux-guerres*, Stichting Kunstboek, Bruges, 1997.

Marguerite Coppens, *Geraardsbergse Chantillykant*, Rotaryclub Ninove / Geraardsbergen, 1984.

Caroline Esgain and Catherine GAUTHIER, *Guide du visiteur de la Chambre des Dentelles*, Musée Mode & Dentelle, Brussels, 2018.

Alice Gandin and Julie ROMAIN (eds), *Dentelles, quand la mode ne tient qu'à un fil* (exh. cat.), Musée de Normandie, Caen, 30 June – 4 November 2012, Somogy, Paris / Caen, 2012.

Anne Kraatz, *Calais, Musée de la Dentelle et de la Mode. Dentelles à la main*, Réunion des Musées Nationaux, Paris, 1996.

Santina M. Levey, *Lace. A History*, Victoria & Albert Museum, Leeds, 1983.

Sylvie Marot (ed.), *Haute dentelle* (exh. cat.), Cité de la dentelle et de la mode à Calais, 9 June 2018 – 6 January 2019, Cité de la mode et de la dentelle / Snoeck, Calais / Ghent, 2018.

COLOPHON

 MARKED is an initiative by Lannoo Publishers.
www.markedbylannoo.com

 JOIN THE MARKED COMMUNITY on
@markedbylannoo

Or sign up for our MARKED newsletter with news about new and forthcoming publications on art, interior design, food & travel, photography and fashion as well as exclusive offers and MARKED events on www.markedbylannoo.com.

Authors: Karen Van Godtsenhoven, Caroline Esgain, Catherine Gauthier & HH Al Reem Al Tenaiji
Editing: Lee Preedy
Translation: Anne Baudouin
Graphic design: Jelle Jespers

If you have any questions or comments about the material in this book, please do not hesitate to contact our editorial team: marked@lannoo.com.

© Lannoo Publishers, Tielt, Belgium, 2019
D/2019/45/477 – NUR 452
ISBN: 978 94 01 46 4703
www.lannoo.com

All rights reserved. No part of this publication may be reproduced or transmitted in any form or by any means, electronic or mechanical, including photocopy, recording or any other information storage and retrieval system, without prior permission in writing from the publisher. Every effort has been made to trace copyright holders. If, however, you feel that you have inadvertently been overlooked, please contact the publishers.

#AREYOUMARKED